STARS AND STRIPES

The Story of the American Flag

BY **Sarah L. Thomson**

★ ★ ★

ILLUSTRATED BY

Bob Dacey and Debra Bandelin

■ HarperCollins*Publishers*

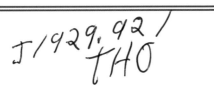
For everyone we lost
—S.L.T.

★

To Ralph Bagley and Kenneth Hine,
with gratitude and admiration for their
passion, integrity, and generosity
—B.D. & D.B.

★

Special thanks to Robert Byrne, Edgar Hayes, Gregg Hansson, Richard Caruso,
and Frank Coughlin of Engine 24, Ladder 5, Greenwich Village, New York City
—B.D. & D.B.

Grateful thanks to Whitney Smith of the Flag Research Center
for his time and expert review

Stars and Stripes: *The Story of the American Flag*
Text copyright © 2003 by Sarah L. Thomson   Illustrations copyright © 2003 by Bob Dacey and Debra Bandelin
Manufactured in China.   All rights reserved.   www.harperchildrens.com

Library of Congress Cataloging-in-Publication Data   Thomson, Sarah L.   Stars and stripes : the story of the American flag / by Sarah L. Thomson ;
illustrated by Bob Dacey and Debra Bandelin.—1st ed.   p.   cm.   Summary: An introduction to the history of the American flag,
from colonial times to the present.   ISBN 0-06-050416-1 — ISBN 0-06-050417-X (lib. bdg.)
1. Flags—United States—History—Juvenile literature.   [1. Flags—United States—History.]   I. Dacey, Bob, ill.
II. Bandelin, Debra, ill.   III. Title.   CR113 .T48   2003   929'.9'2'0973—dc21   2002006377
Typography by Carla Weise   1 2 3 4 5 6 7 8 9 10   ❖   First Edition

Notes on the Flags

Page 7: On July 20, 1969, the flag of the United States was planted on the Sea of Tranquility on the moon.

Page 8: The red-and-white-striped flag is sometimes called the Sons of Liberty Flag. This patriot group first flew a flag with nine red and white stripes but later used one with thirteen stripes, one for each colony.

Page 11: The flag called the Continental Union or the Continental Colors (later known as the Grand Union) was flown near George Washington's camp on Prospect Hill in Somerville, Massachusetts, on January 1, 1776.

Page 12: There were several different rattlesnake flags. The one shown here is called the Gadsden Flag, and it was flown on the *Alfred*, the flagship of the American navy. "Don't" was sometimes spelled without an apostrophe at the time of the Revolutionary War.

Page 17: The resolution passed on June 14, 1777, by the Continental Congress declared "that the flag of the thirteen united States be 13 stripes alternate red and white, that the union be 13 stars, white in a blue field, representing a new constellation." Many different stars and stripes designs were created. Some of the flags shown here include:

The Flag of the Second Regiment Light Dragoons: This flag with blue and silver stripes in the corner was carried during the Revolutionary War.

The *Serapis* Flag: After the *Serapis*, a British ship, was captured by the Americans in 1779, she reportedly flew a flag with thirteen stars and stripes of red, white, and blue.

The Pine Tree Flag: A flag with a pine tree and the motto "An Appeal to Heaven" was flown by some ships of the Massachusetts navy.

The Guilford Courthouse Flag: With blue stars and red and blue stripes, this flag was reportedly carried on the battlefields of North and South Carolina.

Page 18: While Francis Scott Key was on board a British ship in Baltimore Harbor, trying to negotiate the release of a prisoner of war, a battle broke out for possession of Fort McHenry. Key was not allowed to leave the ship while the battle was going on, and he watched the fight from the deck. His poem "The Star-Spangled Banner" was set to a popular tune and immediately became well-known, but it was not made into a national anthem until over a century later, in 1931. The Fort McHenry flag is now preserved in the National Museum of American History in Washington, D.C.

Page 21: There have been no major changes to the United States flag since 1960, one year after Hawaii became a state.

Page 22: The flag shown here is the battle flag of the Confederate Army. It became better known than the official flag of the Confederacy, called the Stars and Bars, which had seven stars in a circle (later the stars increased to thirteen) and three stripes, two red and one white.

The flag of the United States of America has fifty stars and thirteen stripes. People call it the Stars and Stripes.

You can see the flag at schools and at post offices, in town squares, and at baseball games. You can see flags in parades on the Fourth of July.

Every day the Stars and Stripes flies in each of the fifty states. It flies all over the world. It has even flown on the moon.

About two hundred and fifty years ago, America did not have a flag. America was not even a country. It was a group of colonies ruled by England.

Not all Americans wanted to be ruled by England. Some were angry about the taxes England made them pay on things like paper, paint, and tea.

A group of men called the Sons of Liberty sometimes flew a flag to show that they were angry. The flag had thirteen red and white stripes, one for each of the thirteen American colonies.

In 1775 the Revolutionary War began. The American colonies fought to win their freedom from England.

Early in the war the Americans used many different flags.

George Washington commanded the American soldiers. On the first day of 1776, he raised a new flag near his army's camp. The flag had the thirteen red and white stripes that stood for the thirteen colonies. In the corner there was a flag Americans knew well: the flag of England, the Union Jack.

Not all Americans wanted their new flag to show the Union Jack.

Some flew flags with a rattlesnake. The snake came to stand for America. People believed that a rattlesnake would not harm others unless it was threatened. But if it was attacked, it was deadly.

Many flags with the rattlesnake warned: "Don't tread on me."

The Continental Congress was created to govern the American colonies. Two years after the Revolutionary War began, Congress finally decided that America needed a single flag.

The flag would have thirteen stripes, one for each colony. And it would have thirteen stars on a blue background to show that America was a "new constellation," something never seen before.

No one was sure just how the flag should look.

Some flags had red, white, and blue stripes. The stars

might have had five, six, seven, or eight points.

People didn't always have time or even enough

cloth to make a flag carefully. Some flags were stitched

together out of rags and scraps.

The Revolutionary War went on for six long years.

In the end the Americans won. The thirteen colonies

became the United States of America.

Soon two new states, Vermont and Kentucky, joined the United States. Two new stripes and two new stars were added to the flag.

Not long afterward, the United States was again at war with England. This was the War of 1812.

On a September night in 1814, an American lawyer named Francis Scott Key watched English ships attack Fort McHenry in Baltimore Harbor, Maryland. All night long the cannons crashed. In the morning Francis looked up to see if the flag with fifteen stars and stripes was still flying.

It was. Then he knew the Americans had won the battle.

Francis wrote a poem called "The Star-Spangled Banner." Later it became the national anthem of the United States.

More states joined the United States. Sometimes people added a new stripe and a new star to the flag each time. Sometimes they didn't.

In 1818 Congress made a decision. There would only be thirteen stripes in the flag, but there would be a star for every state. Sometimes the stars were in rows, sometimes in circles, and sometimes even in one big star.

Almost a hundred years later, President William Howard Taft decided that the stars should always be in rows. This is how the flag looks today. There are thirteen stripes, seven red and six white, to remind us of the first thirteen colonies. There are fifty stars to tell us that each state in our country is important.

The American flag didn't change even during

the Civil War. In 1861 this terrible war split the United

States into two parts. Eleven southern states tried to

form their own country, the Confederate States of

America.

Some people in the North wanted to take the

stars for the southern states out of the flag. But

President Abraham Lincoln refused. He said that

the United States was still one country.

After four years of fighting, at last the North won.

The country was united again.

The Stars and Stripes has flown when the United

States was at war in lands far away. It has flown on

tanks and on battleships. People put flags in cemeteries

to remember soldiers who have died.

The Stars and Stripes flies in peacetime, too. On special days like Memorial Day and the Fourth of July, people hang flags outside their homes. Sometimes people even wear shirts or jackets or scarves decorated with flags.

The Stars and Stripes hangs behind American athletes who win medals in the Olympic Games.

On September 11, 2001, the United States was attacked. The World Trade Center in New York City was destroyed. A plane hit the Pentagon in Washington, D.C. Another plane crashed in Pennsylvania.

More than three thousand people were killed.

After September 11, Americans flew more flags than ever. They hung flags on homes and stores and office buildings. People wore clothing and jewelry decorated with flags. They flew flags from cars and trucks.

These flags said that, even though people were angry and afraid and very sad, they still had hope and faith in their country.

No matter what happened, they believed the Stars and Stripes would always keep flying.

What About Betsy Ross?

Many people think that Betsy Ross sewed the first American flag. But history shows that this probably isn't true.

Elizabeth Ross was a seamstress who lived in Philadelphia, Pennsylvania. She told her family that, during the Revolutionary War, George Washington and two other men asked her to sew a national flag. Following their design and adding some ideas of her own, she sewed the first Stars and Stripes.

Elizabeth Ross's grandson thought that the meeting took place in 1776. But this doesn't seem possible. The Continental Congress didn't choose the Stars and Stripes design for the flag until 1777. There is no record of Congress ever appointing a committee to select a flag. And George Washington didn't write about it in any of his letters or diaries.

Elizabeth Ross did make "colors," or flags, for the Pennsylvania ships that were part of the American navy. But there is no real reason to think that she ever sewed a national flag.

The truth is that we don't know who made the first flag with the stars and stripes. Perhaps it was done in a house like Elizabeth Ross's, or maybe in a fort or a military camp. It may have been stitched up in a hurry or patched together from scraps. The person who created it probably had no idea how important that flag would be, and that in time it would be recognized all over the world.

—S.L.T.